Genre > **Biography**

Essential Question
How can one person make a difference?

Jacob Riis
Champion of the Poor

by Sarah Wilcox

Chapter 1 Beginnings	2
Chapter 2 A New Tool	8
Chapter 3 Showing the Slums	12
Respond to Reading	15
PAIRED READ The Fight for Equality	16
Glossary/Index	19
Focus on Social Studies	20

CHAPTER 1

Beginnings

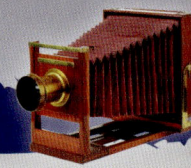

Jacob Riis (*REES*) **immigrated** to the United States in the 1870s. Many people came to New York City at that time for a better life. Instead, they had to live in crowded **slums**.

Riis wanted people to **understand** how hard life was for new immigrants.

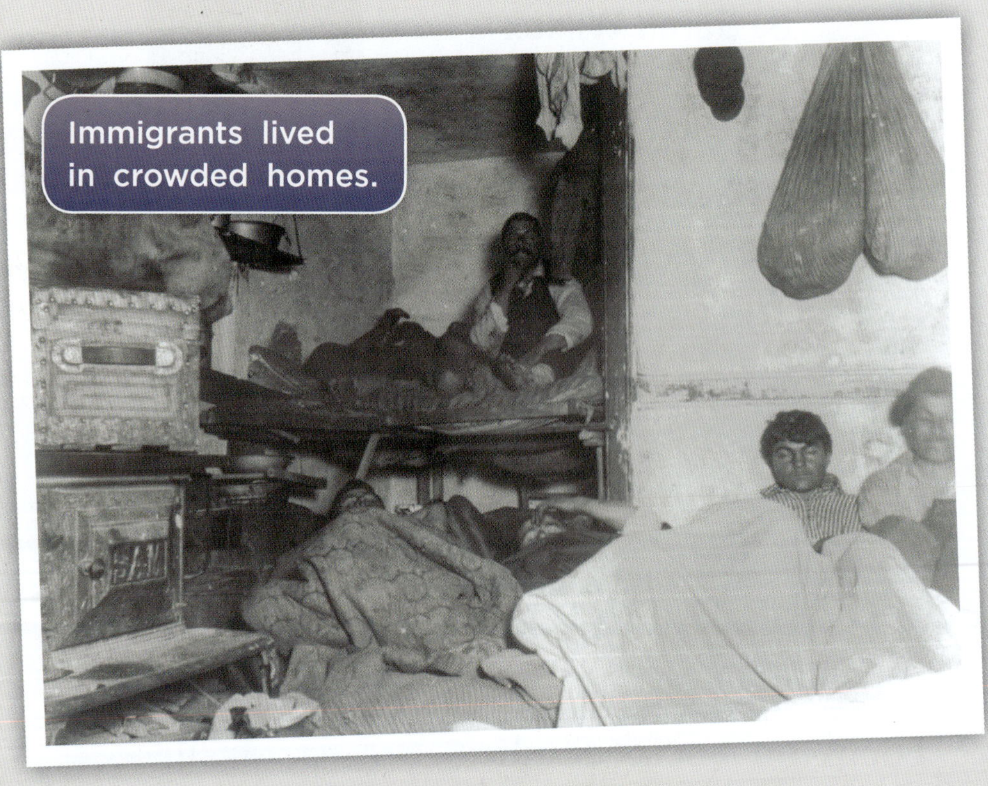

Immigrants lived in crowded homes.

(tr) D. Hurst/Alamy, (b) Library of Congress, Prints & Photographs Division [LC-USZ62-16348]

Riis became a reporter. He wrote stories about the lives of immigrants. He also took photographs. His stories and photos showed what life was like in the slums. They helped make life better for the poor.

Many children lived in slums in New York City.

Jacob Riis was born in 1849 in Denmark. He learned English in school and became a carpenter.

Riis met a young woman named Elisabeth Nielsen. He wanted to marry her, but first he needed a job. Riis could not find work, so he went to the United States to look for a job.

STOP AND CHECK

Why did Jacob Riis move to the United States?

From Denmark to the United States

New York

UNITED STATES

Riis traveled to the United States by sea.

Riis arrived in New York City in 1870. He worked as a carpenter and on the railroad. He wrote stories for magazines.

Sometimes, Riis was **mistreated**. His employers gave him less money than they had **agreed**, or said they would pay him. Sometimes, he didn't have enough money for food or a place to sleep.

Riis was still poor after three years. He needed money so he could he **fulfill** his dream of marrying Elisabeth.

There were many immigrants in New York City like Riis. Most were not qualified to do jobs that paid well. The immigrants lived in buildings called tenements. The tenements were cramped and crowded with too many people. Sometimes 15 people lived in one room. Many rooms were underground. There was no light or fresh air.

Immigrants lived in tenements like this one.

MANY IMMIGRANTS

Huge numbers of people immigrated to the United States from 1847 to 1930. They came from countries such as Ireland and Germany.

Other immigrants lived under bridges. Jacob Riis wrote, "No pig would have been content to live in such a place."

A very poor area in New York City was Five Points. Many people there did not have jobs. Most children were too dirty and hungry to go to school.

STOP AND CHECK

What was life like for immigrants in New York City?

Many people in Five Points lived in sheds.

CHAPTER 2
A New Tool

Riis got a job as a reporter in 1873. He wrote about the terrible **conditions** poor people lived in. Riis felt that this was an <mark>injustice</mark>.

Now that Riis had a job, he went back to Denmark to marry Elisabeth. Then they came back to New York together.

This photograph is of Elisabeth Riis and their son Edward.

Riis kept writing about **poverty**. He believed that poor people committed crimes because of their living conditions. Riis needed to convince readers about the poor living conditions. He thought if people saw what the slums were really like, then they would believe his stories.

In 1887, Riis read about a new way to take photos in the dark. Photographers used powder to make a bright light. It was called flash photography.

Before this, it was only possible to take photos during the day. Riis thought that he could use this new photography to take photos inside the slums and at night. Then he would be able to show what the slums were really like.

> **STOP AND CHECK**
>
> How could photographers take pictures of dark spaces?

Riis bought a camera and a flash. He began using flash photography in 1888.

Flash photography was dangerous. One time the flash powder **exploded** in Riis's face. He was wearing glasses, so his eyes were not hurt.

> **STOP AND CHECK**
>
> How did flash photography help Jacob Riis?

Riis took photos of children sleeping on the streets.

USING FLASH PHOTOGRAPHY

1. Riis put his camera on a tripod.

2. Then he ground the two flash powders **separately**, or one by one.

3. Next, he mixed the powders together.

4. Then he threw a match on the flash powder. He didn't get too close!

5. Riis took the photo. The flash lit up the scene.

A photographer lights the flash powder.

CHAPTER 3
Showing the Slums

The photos Riis took and his stories were printed in newspapers. The photos shocked people. Riis told people that immigrants needed better places to live.

In 1890, Riis published a book called *How the Other Half Lives*. It showed what the slums were like.

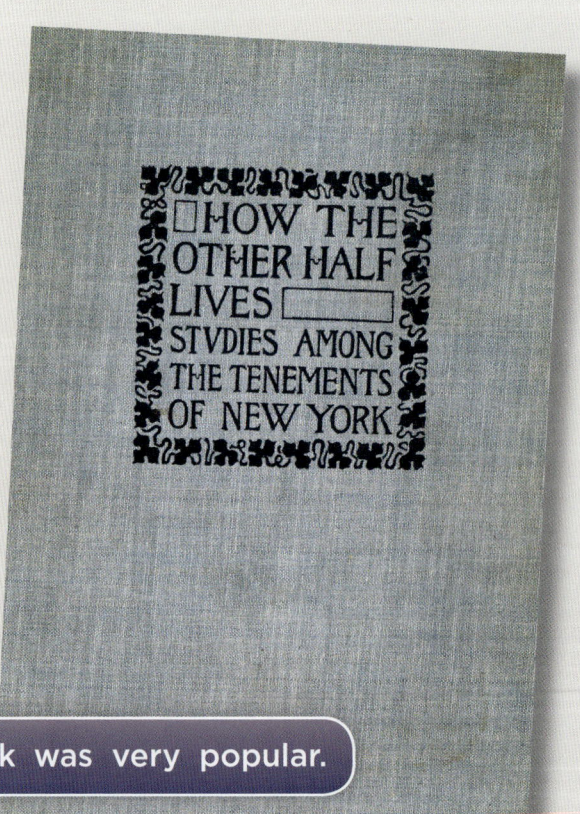

Riis's book was very popular.

Riis took this photo of men sleeping on the floor.

The future president, Theodore Roosevelt, read Riis's book. He gave Riis a lot of **encouragement**.

Riis's book encouraged the city council to improve living conditions for the poor. The city began to clean up the Five Points slum.

It took 14 years to tear down the Five Points slum. Riis's work helped to **accomplish** that task.

Jacob Riis died in 1914. Jacob Riis Park in New York City is a **memorial** to him.

STOP AND CHECK

What important things did Jacob Riis do?

People enjoy the beach at Jacob Riis Park.

THE LIFE OF JACOB RIIS

1849: Riis is born in Ribe, Denmark.
1870: Riis immigrates to the United States.
1873: Riis begins working as a newspaper reporter.
1876: Riis marries Elisabeth Nielsen.
1888: Riis first uses flash photography.
1890: Riis publishes the book *How the Other Half Lives*.
1914: Riis dies.

Summarize

Summarize how Jacob Riis helped the poor. Your graphic organizer may help.

Text Evidence

1. Reread Chapter 1. What does the author think of living conditions in the slums? Use details from the text to show the author's point of view. **AUTHOR'S POINT OF VIEW**

2. Find the word *convince* on page 9. What clues in the paragraph help you figure out its meaning? **VOCABULARY**

3. Write about how Jacob Riis made a difference. Use details from the text to support your answer. **WRITE ABOUT READING**

Genre Biography

Compare Texts
Read about how a young girl made a difference in her community.

The Fight for Equality

Sylvia Mendez grew up in California in the 1940s. Non-white children had to go to different schools from white children then.

Sylvia's parents tried to **register** her at a school for white children. Sylvia's father was from Mexico. Her mother was from Puerto Rico. Sylvia wasn't allowed to go to the white school. The school for non-white children was older and farther away from the white school.

16

Martin H. Simon/CORBIS

Victory!

Sylvia's parents thought she should be able to go to the white school. Her parents and the community **protested**. They sued the school district and won.

After this, California was the first state to end school **segregation** in 1947. People in other states began to protest, too. They held **boycotts**. By 1969, children of different races could go to the same school.

These people are protesting against school segregation.

Life After School

Sylvia went to the school for white children. She worked hard.

Today, Sylvia Mendez speaks at schools. She encourages students to study.

Mendez was awarded the Presidential Medal of Freedom in 2011. The medal is for her work for **civil rights**. It is given to people who make a difference.

President Barack Obama gives Sylvia her medal.

Make Connections

How did Sylvia Mendez make a difference?
ESSENTIAL QUESTION

Jacob Riis and Sylvia Mendez both made a difference in their communities. How are they the same? How are they different? **TEXT TO TEXT**

Glossary

civil rights *(SI-vuhl rights)* the rights of people no matter what their race is *(page 18)*

conditions *(kuhn-DI-shuhnz)* what places are like *(page 8)*

immigrated *(I-muh-grayt-uhd)* moved to a new country *(page 2)*

poverty *(PO-vur-tee)* experience of being poor *(page 9)*

segregation *(se-gruh-GAY-shuhn)* separating by race *(page 17)*

slums *(sluhmz)* rundown areas where poor people live *(page 2)*

Index

Five Points, 7, 13

flash photography, 9, 10, 11, 14

How the Other Half Lives, 12–14

Nielsen, Elisabeth, 4, 5, 8, 14

Presidential Medal of Freedom, 18

Roosevelt, Theodore, 13

Focus on Social Studies

Purpose To show how kids can make a difference in their communities

Procedure

Step 1 Work with a partner or in a small group. Brainstorm things you would like to change in your community.

Step 2 Choose one thing you would most like to do something about.

Step 3 Make a plan. What are you going to do? How will you do it? Who is going to do what? What help will you need?

Step 4 Share your plan with the rest of the class.